D0549087

OUR LOVE OF
Hummingbirds

Stan Tekiela

Adventure Publications
Cambridge, Minnesota

Dedication

To Kathy. You are my blue sky and sunshine.

Edited by Sandy Livoti

Cover and book design by Lora Westberg

Front cover: female Ruby-throated Hummingbird; back cover: male Ruby-throated Hummingbird

All photos by Stan Tekiela

10 9 8 7 6 5 4 3 2 1

Copyright 2017 by Stan Tekiela
Published by Adventure Publications, an imprint of AdventureKEEN
820 Cleveland Street South
Cambridge, Minnesota 55008
(800) 678-7006
www.adventurepublications.net
Printed in China
ISBN: 978-1-59193-688-6; eISBN: 978-1-59193-689-3

Symbol of Fancy and Fun in the Garden

Hummingbirds are some of the most fanciful and fun birds to see! They are unique in so many ways—from their fast flight and sparkling colors to their extraordinary abilities and unusual behaviors. Of all the birds that come to my yard, I especially enjoy the hummers. I look forward to their return from the tropics in spring and enjoy their amazing in-flight acrobatics all summer long. When they leave to fly south in the fall, it's like saying farewell to close friends. It's true that I love all birds, but if I were pressed to pick a top choice, it would be hummingbirds. These radiant little birds have captured my heart, and I'm sure they will quickly catch yours, too.

Spring Arrives:
Where Are My Hummingbirds?

Weeks after the weather warms, Ruby-throated Hummingbirds are still nowhere to be found. The journey northward is long and difficult for these winged jewels. Like many small birds, they migrate at night and feed during the day. Tiny Ruby-throats are no match for the strong winds blasting out of the north or large storms whipping in the Gulf of Mexico during spring migration, so they wait for the favorable, warm southern winds to help propel them along.

Along with the weather, wildflowers and insects also play a role in migration. If Ruby-throats migrate before wildflower nectar is readily available or insect populations hatch, they can starve to death. When all of the conditions are in place at the proper time, one spring morning you will awake to find your hummingbirds home again.

Home After a Long Flight

There is a special joy in seeing our hummingbirds return from the tropics each spring. People who put out hummingbird feeders are especially thankful that the birds survived the long flight from the wintering grounds, in some cases up to 2,000 miles away!

Hummingbirds, such as the Broad-tailed, enjoy the good life during the winter months, feeding from a profusion of tropical flowers. These months are a time of rest and recuperation, and that includes a hiatus from breeding. They won't mate and raise young again until they come back to our yards. This makes the habitat we provide for them very important indeed.

Typically, the male hummers return a few days to a week before the females. Depending on the weather, sometimes they all arrive at the same time.

Are These My Hummers?

If you forget to put out your feeders early enough in spring, your hummingbirds will let you know they clearly have arrived. They will zip and zoom around the exact sites of the feeders from the previous year, looking for the same food sources they obviously remember well. So it's time to get your feeders out—now.

Studies of birds, including some of hummers, such as Black-chinned Hummingbirds, show that if they are successful at raising young in a particular area in one year, they will return to it to breed in the following year. In addition, the offspring from the previous year tend to return to the same general area where they hatched, making it extremely likely that the hummers you're seeing now are the same ones you came to know before—a very comforting thought!

Independence in Territories

Hummingbirds are very different from many other bird species. While countless numbers of birds form long-term bonds with their mates, all hummingbirds, including Magnificent Hummingbirds, never do this. In fact, after briefly courting and breeding, males and females go their separate ways and have nothing to do with each other as partners anymore.

After arriving in spring, both male and female hummers set up their own territories. Sometimes their sites are adjacent. Other times, the boundaries overlap. In any situation, each hummingbird vigorously defends its home range of about ½–1 acre.

The More Hummers, the Better!

Hummingbirds don't live long—only about 3–5 years on average. With such short life spans, they must start mating the first spring after they hatch and be successful at reproduction, or their population will plummet.

Hummers produce only 2 babies each year, and typically just 1 survives. The surviving baby represents the eventual replacement of one of the parents, but it doesn't increase the population. If the second year of breeding produces another surviving offspring, ultimately both parents will be replaced, but this still doesn't boost the population. It is only in the third year of successful breeding that hummingbirds start adding to their overall ranks.

Where's the Food?

It takes a delicate balance of good weather and an abundance of flowers and insects to keep our hummingbirds healthy and thriving. Areas with a reliable food source, such as a generous patch of wildflowers or a large flower garden in your yard, directly impact where a hummingbird will lay claim to a territory.

Hummingbird feeders can also influence where hummers will set up shop for the summer. So if you want more of these fantastic birds around your home, consider putting up another nectar feeder or planting more kinds of flowers that hummingbirds like.

Clever Nest Sites

Once territories are established, the female selects a nest site on top of a flexible twig or a hanging branch that's less than 2 inches wide. Sometimes she constructs a nest on an impossibly thin clothesline, or even an electrical wire! Other times she builds a nest only to abandon it and start another a short distance away. Occasionally she will fix up and reuse her nest from the previous year.

A hummingbird nest is very tiny—a Ruby-throat's is not much larger than half of a walnut shell. The intricate, miniature structure takes 6–10 days to build, depending on the female's experience and available nesting materials.

The Incredible, Flexible Nest

Now the female flies back and forth, gathering the "building blocks" for her nest—small bits of soft plants, such as cottonwood seed fluff and grapevine strips. She glues the nest's base to the foundation and fastens the materials together with spider silk, which she collects separately. Often she will simply fly through spider webs, collecting them on her chest for easy transport. Look closely at your female Ruby-throats during spring and you might spot some strands of spider silk on them.

Next, she lines the interior with the softest materials and forms the cup with her body to seal out rain and hold in heat. Finally, she pastes tiny bits of lichen to the exterior, blending it into the surroundings.

The finished nest fits her snugly, but the fit can be tight if both babies hatch and survive. Fortunately, the spider webs allow the nest to expand as the chicks grow.

Solo Incubation, Day and Night

During nest building, the female leaves her territory to seek out a male for mating. After breeding, she lays two tiny white-to-cream eggs that are no bigger than a pea. She incubates the eggs for the next 14–16 days and nights, sitting on them to keep them warm, usually at about 99 °F. She leaves the nest every 10–20 minutes or so to feed and defecate. When she returns, she uses her long, pointed bill to turn the eggs over a few times. Because the nest cup is shaped specifically for her body, she usually faces the same direction when she settles down to incubate again.

Hungry, Helpless Babies

Once the chicks hatch, the mother gets busy feeding them. Her hatchlings are naked, with their eyes closed and ears sealed shut. Raising their heads instinctively, they open their short, tiny beaks to be fed. The mother complies, regurgitating a liquid directly into their mouths by sliding her long bill down their throats to pass along the food. As the babies grow, each feeding session looks more like a sword-swallowing act. After just a few days, the babies open their eyes and start to grow feathers.

Parenting Is Hard Work!

Mother hummingbirds are totally dedicated to raising their young. After all, being a single parent is never easy, especially with a couple of hungry mouths to feed. At this time the mother is fully committed to collecting enough nectar and protein-packed insects for her young. She will go out to gather food several times per hour, all day long, day after day.

Thankfully, the babies grow quickly. By 15–25 days of age, the babies are large enough to leave the nest. Called fledglings now, when they fly out from the edge of the nest for the first time, they don't come back. Compared with many other bird species, the process from hatching to leaving the nest (fledging) goes rather quickly.

Feeding Outside the Nest

Hummers eat a lot and spend much of their day searching for food and feeding. You might notice much more activity at your hummingbird feeders at this time, because the juveniles have joined the adult females and swarm around the food.

The metabolism of a hummingbird is roughly 100 times that of an elephant! To maintain the energy to keep moving, each day the hummer needs to consume enough food to equal about 1½–3 times its own body weight. Hummers can't survive on the sugar water (nectar) in feeders alone. A big part of their diet is tiny insects. Eating insects is how they get all the vitamins, minerals and critical nutrients necessary for a healthy life.

A hummer will sit on a branch, waiting for an insect to fly by, and then zip out to snatch it from the air. Another common feeding technique is to visit spider webs and pluck out the insects stuck in the silk, eating one bug right after another.

Are They Really Green?

Many hummer species, such as Broad-billed Hummingbirds, are mostly green in color. Usually the head, neck and back are green and the rest of the body color varies from species to species. Unlike cardinals, which have a pigment that colors their feathers red, a pigment doesn't cause the green color in hummers. No, we see green because of tiny cells in the barbs of feathers that absorb the available daylight and reflect only the green wavelength of light back to our eyes. While a prism breaks down daylight into the full spectrum of light, feathers on the head, neck and back of most hummingbird species absorb the rainbow colors except for the green range. Depending on the amount of light being reflected, our little friends shine like green beacons on sunny days and appear duller green on cloudy days.

What? No Speeding Ticket?

The eyesight of hummingbirds is excellent. In fact, they depend on their sense of sight because it's the only way they find their food. They see in the same full-color spectrum that we see, but they can also see beyond what we see.

Hummers can see a tiny splash of color from a great distance or while flying at high speeds—which is why they can zip by a colorful small flower and zero in on it. It's also why you don't need to add red food coloring to your nectar feeder. Any amount of red on a feeder is enough to attract hummers.

Their vision has to be good to avoid dangerous twigs and sticks while they dash through the forest. Hummers can't afford to hit objects like these and break a wing. Not only do they need to see obstacles, but they must also react fast enough to maintain a safe flight. When you think about it, everything hummingbirds do is fast.

Up, Down, or Upside Down

Hummingbirds get their common name from the humming sound that their wings make while flapping. To make such a noise, the wings must move very fast. During an average flight, hummers flap their wings about 70–80 times per second. That's right—per second. During courtship flights, when a male is trying to impress a female, he flaps his wings at an incredible 250 times per second!

Most birds have flexible wings and flap in an up-and-down manner. Hummingbirds are very different, with fused wings that work more like a stiff board. They flap in a figure-eight pattern, rather than up and down. This means that hummers have a power stroke on both the upward and downward flaps, which more than doubles the effectiveness of their moving wings. It also allows the birds to hover, and even fly backward and upside down!

Cling—Then Fly!

A hummingbird's foot is like that of many other birds: 3 toes point forward and 1 points back. On each toe are tiny nails, called talons. Hummers don't do much walking. It's easier for them to quickly flap their wings, spin around and land where they want. But make no mistake—their feet work very well. They have excellent grip strength, which allows them to cling tightly to a perch whether they're at rest or on the lookout.

Food Fights and Squabbles

The number of hummingbird visits to your nectar feeders increases dramatically in late summer, as do the fights and squabbles for the food. At this time, both adult and juvenile hummers, such as Blue-throated Hummingbirds, crowd around the feeders in hopes of getting their turn. It is generally accepted that a rich, consistent food source, such as a nectar feeder, is well worth fighting for or trying to defend. A good way to mediate the increased fighting before migration is to put out more feeders and space them farther apart.

Fat for the Journey

A typical male Ruby-throated Hummingbird weighs about 2.5 grams. In preparation for migration, these hummers go into a hyperphagia stage, or feeding frenzy, causing them to nearly double their weight in fat. This fat fuels the long migratory flight ahead. Most hummers can fly about 250 miles per night. They rest the next day and continue to feed in the hyperphagia mode, replacing what they burned up overnight.

It's been calculated that doubling their body fat allows hummers to fly upwards of 600 miles nonstop. This is important because at the U.S. southern border, these tiny birds must fly over the Gulf of Mexico to the Yucatan Peninsula in Mexico, with no place to rest in between.

Each bird migrates alone. The first hummers to leave in autumn are the adult males. They usually start heading out by the end of August and the beginning of September. Shortly after, adult females begin their flight south. Last, the young hummers migrate. How they know where to go and the way to get there is still a natural history mystery—but they do it, and they are successful.

Nectar Feeders for the Migrators

Hummingbirds migrate in response to a hormone surge triggered by the length of daylight, called the photoperiod. The timing of migration is not a matter of choice for birds. Nothing you can do will stop them from migrating, so it's not necessary to take down your feeders to "jump-start" hummingbirds to start flying south.

Hummingbirds require extra food to prepare for the journey ahead, so your feeders are more important than ever. Also, hummers that live north of you will take advantage of nectar feeders as they move through your region. In fact, your feeders may be the food source that saves a struggling hummer in its time of need. So it's best to leave the feeders up for another several weeks after you've last seen any hummingbirds.

Where Are They During Winter?

For well over half of the year, most of our hummingbirds are migrating and spending the winter in the tropics. In fact, in most of the United States and Canada, they only spend about 3–4 months visiting our backyards. The Rufous Hummingbird migrates the farthest, with some flying from as far north as Alaska down to the tropics. The Ruby-throated Hummingbird—the only hummer species in the eastern half of the country—migrates to Mexico and Central America. Some spend the winter along the Gulf Coast, but the vast majority head for tropical habitats south of the U.S. border.

In Our Hearts Until They Return

One morning you wake up to a quiet stillness around the nectar feeders. The hummers are no longer zipping around the yard, and the familiar buzzing of their tiny wings has stopped. Before the first autumn frost kills the flowers, our jeweled birds have moved south to get to warmer weather.

With the end of summer in the north and the cycle of reproduction completed, it's like a switch has been flipped, signaling that it's time to leave. Soon winter will begin, and we'll hold the hummers in our memories until next spring. One day, well after the weather has warmed and the flowers are blooming, our hummingbirds will return to our yards to warm and delight our hearts once again.

Observation Notes

Date:

Date:

About the Author

Naturalist, wildlife photographer and writer Stan Tekiela is the author of the popular Our Love of Wildlife book series that includes *Our Love of Moose* and *Our Love of Loons*. He has authored more than 165 field guides, nature books, children's books, wildlife audio CDs, puzzles and playing cards, presenting many species of birds, mammals, reptiles, amphibians, trees, wildflowers and cacti in the United States.

With a Bachelor of Science degree in Natural History from the University of Minnesota and as an active professional naturalist for more than 25 years, Stan studies and photographs wildlife throughout the United States and Canada. He has received various national and regional awards for his books and photographs. Also a well-known columnist and radio personality, his syndicated column appears in more than 25 newspapers and his wildlife programs are broadcast on a number of Midwest radio stations. Stan can be followed on Facebook and Twitter. He can be contacted via www.naturesmart.com.